Student Guide to the
Sarbanes-Oxley Act

Robert Prentice

Thomson Publishing
5191 Natorp Blvd
Mason, Ohio 45040
USA

For information about our products,
contact us:
**Thomson Learning Academic Resource
Center**
1-800-423-0563
http://www.swcollege.com

International Headquarters
Thomson Learning
International Division
290 Harbor Drive, 2nd Floor
Stamford, CT 06902-7477
USA

UK/Europe/Middle East/South Af
Thomson Learning
Berkshire House
168-173 High Holborn
London WCIV 7AA
United Kingdom

Asia
Thomson Learning
60 Albert Street, #15-01
Albert Complex
Singapore 189969

Canada
Nelson Thomson Learning
1120 Birchmount Road
Toronto, Ontario MIK 5G4
Canada

ISBN 978-0-324-32365-8

ISBN 0-324-32365-4

The Adaptable Courseware Program consists of products and additions to existing Brooks
products that are produced from camera-ready copy. Peer review, class testing, and accur
are primarily the responsibility of the author(s).

INTRODUCTION

The Enron era's financial debacle was the greatest business scandal of a generation and one of the biggest of the last century. Once the seventh largest company on the Fortune 500, Enron took bankruptcy and essentially blinked out of existence following a wave of revelations of accounting regularities and securities fraud. Headlines soon linked Global Crossing, Tyco, WorldCom, Adelphia, HealthSouth and other companies to similar frauds, prompting Congress in June 2002 to pass the **Sarbanes-Oxley Act (SOX),** the most significant securities law changes since passage of the original federal securities laws in 1933 and 1934.

Containing provisions to create a new federal agency, restructure the entire accounting industry, reform Wall Street practices, dramatically alter corporate governance practices here and abroad, attack insider trading and obstruction of justice, Sarbanes-Oxley could ultimately prove to be one of America's most significant economic regulations. In the two plus years since it was enacted, much has happened. The Public Company Accounting Oversight Board (PCAOB) has come into being. The PCAOB and the Securities Exchange Commission (SEC) have issued countless rules to implement Sarbanes-Oxley's many legislative mandates. Some of Sarbanes-Oxley's rules took effect almost immediately. Others have kicked in over time and a few are not yet in force. Although the PCAOB and SEC will be issuing many new rules over the next few years to fully realize what Congress has envisioned, Sarbanes-Oxley is largely implemented. Since its passage, it has remained topic number one in corporate boardrooms and accounting offices across the world, on Wall Street, and in executive education programs and other business classrooms. Everyone in business or hoping to enter business will profit by having a clearer understanding of this landmark law.

Most of Sarbanes-Oxley's provisions were aimed at solving specific deficiencies in auditing practice, corporate governance, and capital markets that Congress believed existed. Securities fraud was rife. Financial statements were

1

wildly erroneous.   Gatekeepers such as auditors, directors, attorneys, and securities analysts were found wanting.   This book initially presents an executive summary of SOX's provisions.   Then, after outlining SOX by presenting its table of contents, the book examines Sarbanes-Oxley section-by-section to explain what *problem* Congress was addressing in each section, the *solution* Congress chose, and the *implications and consequences* of the new statute indicated by two years of experience.   **It focuses on what Sarbanes-Oxley means for business *now*.**

EXECUTIVE SUMMARY

Sarbanes-Oxley is a complex and wide-ranging statute, deserving section-by-section analysis. However, an executive summary of its provisions looks like this:

Accounting Reforms. Sarbanes-Oxley replaced the audit industry's self-regulation with a new federal agency, the PCAOB, which will register, inspect, and discipline American and foreign accounting firms that audit public companies accessing American capital markets. It will also establish or supervise the establishment of accounting, auditing, and ethical standards.

To increase the independence of auditors, SOX forbids auditors of public firms from providing to their audit clients most nonaudit consulting services, although provision of tax services has not yet been banned. Permitted nonaudit services must be preapproved by the client's audit committee. Partners in charge of audit clients and reviewing partners must be rotated on a 5-years-on, 5-years-off basis, and other partners on a 7-2-7 basis. Auditors face a one-year "cooling off" period before going to work for the audit client in a key position. Auditors can no longer be compensated for selling consulting services to audit clients, and must retain audit workpapers for seven years.

The SEC. SOX enlarges the SEC's budget and grants it new authority and powers, such as the ability to temporarily or permanently ban individuals from being officers or directors of public companies without court order and the power to freeze accounts to ensure that wrongdoers do not make off with funds while an investigation is underway. The SEC has been substantially more active since June 2002.

Financial Reporting. SOX contains two provisions requiring CEOs and CFOs to certify that to the best of their knowledge the filings their companies make with the SEC are accurate. One of the provisions carries substantial criminal penalties. To ensure that their opinions are based upon reliable information, these officers must also certify that they have put into place internal financial controls. Those controls are audited by the outside auditors, just as are the financial statements. Establishment, evaluation, operation, and documentation of these internal controls have proven to be costly for many companies. Furthermore, new rules restricting off-balance sheet reporting, use of special purpose entities, and pro forma reporting aim to improve the accuracy of financial statements.

Corporate Governance. SOX requires that public companies have audit committees composed entirely of independent directors and containing at least one financial expert. These audit committees have important new responsibilities, including (a) authority to select, evaluate, compensate, and terminate their firms' outside auditors, (b) responsibility to receive communications from auditors about key accounting issues, and (c) obligation to establish procedures to process the complaints of whistleblowers. Until Sarbanes-Oxley, corporate governance was primarily the province of state legislatures and courts. SOX's provisions change this forever, making the federal government a major player in shaping corporate governance.

Wall Street Practices. SOX reforms stock analyst practices, primarily by minimizing in several ways the motivations they previously had to falsely praise the stocks of companies whose investment banking business their employers sought. For example, stock analysts can no longer be compensated on the basis of how much investment banking revenue they generate for their firms, nor can investment bankers be given veto power over their recommendations.

Securities Fraud. SOX creates an entirely new securities fraud crime and a new crime for *conspiring* to commit securities fraud, substantially increases the penalties for several existing securities fraud crimes, lengthens the statute of limitations for civil damages actions for securities fraud, and directs the United States Sentencing Commission to amend sentencing guidelines to deal more harshly with securities fraud and related wrongs.

Officer Conduct. SOX requires companies to install a code of ethics for top financial officers, or explain why they have not done so. It prohibits public companies from lending money to top officers and directors and requires insiders to report their trades in their own companies' stock more promptly than before and to forfeit performance-based bonuses when the financial statements upon which the bonuses were based are later restated due to "wrongful actions." They must also forfeit profits made when selling shares at inflated prices that later drop when financial statements are restated. And they must forfeit profits earned or losses avoided when trading during pension plan "blackout" periods when lower level employees are prevented from trading.

Document Destruction. Sarbanes-Oxley creates three new provisions to punish destruction of evidence that might be helpful in a federal investigation. No grand jury need be convened nor charges pending for them to apply. As noted earlier, one provision requires auditors to preserve their workpapers for seven years after completing the audit.

Whistleblowers. Sarbanes-Oxley not only directs audit committees to install procedures for ensuring that whistleblowers' complaints are properly directed, it also creates a civil cause of action for some whistleblowers who are punished and establishes a new federal crime to punish those who wrongfully retaliate against whistleblowers. The criminal provision is not limited to securities crimes or to public companies.

Attorneys. Sarbanes-Oxley places limited responsibilities upon attorneys for public companies to report "up the line," perhaps as far as the board of directors, when they learn of fraudulent corporate activity by their clients' employees.

International Ramifications. Because 1,450 or so foreign public companies access American securities markets, Congress made most of Sarbanes-Oxley's provisions, including those regarding corporate governance practices, applicable to them. And because foreign accounting firms audit most of these companies, SOX requires those firms to register with the PCAOB and makes them potentially subject to significant American regulation. Controversy continues to flare over this extraterritorial application of American law.

TABLE OF CONTENTS OF SARBANES-OXLEY

SECTION-BY-SECTION ANALYSIS

We now proceed to a section-by-section analysis of Sarbanes-Oxley's many and varied provisions.

PART ONE: ACCOUNTING REFORM

During the 1990s as the economy rolled and the dot.com boom got underway, many thought they detected disconcerting trends in the public accounting profession. Signs of earnings management appeared everywhere. Many observers have argued that some corporate executives and audit partners likely thought that government was not serious about enforcing SEC reporting rules. Congress had passed a 1995 statute making it more difficult for investors to sue for securities fraud and SEC attempts to reform the audit industry had been defeated by congressional pressure at the instance of accounting firm lobbyists. Whatever the reason, corporate misreporting seems to have skyrocketed in the 1990s. Many companies were able to cover up their misdeeds during the rapid ballooning of the dot.com bubble; but when the bubble began to deflate, many chickens came home to roost.

Earnings restatements by publicly held companies spiked from an average of 49 per year from 1990-1997 to 91 in 1998, 150 in 1999, and 156 in 2000, to 270 in 2001 to 330 in 2002. About 10% of all public U.S. companies restated their financials at least once between 1997 and June 2000, and it is recognized that other poor quality audits likely did not come to light if the clients did not suffer financial difficulties.

Although Enron became the poster child for the scams of the dot.com era, it had substantial company. HealthSouth overstated its earnings by $4.6 billion dollars, while Adelphia hid more than $2 billion in debt. WorldCom inflated its earnings by $11 billion and wiped out $180 billion in shareholder wealth when fraud disclosures collapsed its stock, while its industry competitor Global Crossing collapsed under $12.4 billion in hidden debt. Disclosure of Tyco's accounting fraud cost investors over $100 billion. Xerox incorrectly booked $6.4 billion in revenue. Write-offs of

$148 billion erased virtually all of the profits reported by NASDAQ companies between 1995 and 2000. All in all, stock wealth collapsed by *six trillion dollars* with the collapse of the dot.com bubble. These are huge, nearly incomprehensible inaccuracies. How did the auditors get it so wrong?

Whatever the explanation, Congress decided that action had to be taken, creating a new regulatory agency in Title I of Sarbanes-Oxley, and shoring up auditor independence in Title II.

Title I. Public Company Accounting Oversight Board

Sections 101-109

The Problem. In creating the PCAOB, Congress was addressing the failure of the accounting industry's self-regulation model. Throughout the 1990s, the Big Six (then Big Five... and now Big Four) strived in every way conceivable to increase their streams of revenue, paying little attention to the public trust. Public company auditors, who were supposed to be watchdogs for the public interest, became advocates for their audit clients in an attempt to curry favor in order to sell more consulting services. Although most accountants were honorable and most audits were professionally done, a not insignificant number of auditors resigned in disgust at the deemphasizing of professional audit standards at their firms.

The Solution. Section 101 of SOX's Title I establishes the Public Company Accounting Oversight Board as an independent, non-profit body "to oversee the audit of public companies that are subject to the securities laws, and related matters, in order to protect the interests of investors and further the public interest in the preparation of informative, accurate, and independent audit reports for" public companies. The SEC appoints the Board's members and exercises oversight and enforcement authority over it.

Section 101 grants the PCAOB, subject to SEC supervision, authority to (1) register public accounting firms that prepare audit reports for issuers; (2) establish, adopt, or both, auditing, quality control, ethics, independence, and other standards; (3) conduct inspections of registered public accounting firms; and (4) conduct investigations and disciplinary proceedings and, where justified impose appropriate sanctions upon auditors and audit firms.

To effectuate the Board's authority to register public accounting firms, Section 102 provides for mandatory registration of public accounting firms and makes it unlawful for any person who is not registered to prepare, issue, or even to participate in the preparation or issuance of any audit report regarding a public company. Required disclosures include information relating to criminal, civil, or disciplinary proceedings pending against the firm of its auditors in connection with any audit report.

Section 103 orders the PCAOB to establish by rule auditing, quality control, and ethics standards as necessary or appropriate in the public interest or to otherwise protect investors. The Board is authorized to adopt standards issued by professional groups of accountants, such as the AICPA or FASB (Financial Accounting Standards Board—the body most responsible for setting accounting standards in recent years), but is ordered to retain full authority to modify, supplement, revise, amend, or repeal those standards. In other words, the buck stops with the PCAOB, even though this section orders it to cooperate on an ongoing basis with professional groups of accountants. The PCAOB has begun issuing new audit standards, but the SEC seems content at the moment to rely upon the FASB for accounting standards.

Section 104 orders the PCAOB to conduct continuing inspections of public accounting firms to assess their compliance with Sarbanes-Oxley, with PCAOB and SEC rules, and with professional standards as they all relate to audits of public companies. Firms that conduct audits of more than 100 public companies must be inspected annually. Firms conducting fewer audits must be inspected at least once every three years. Decisions are reviewable by the SEC.

Section 105 instructs the Board to establish fair procedures for investigations and disciplining of registered public accounting firms and their accountants. It grants the agency broad authority to require testimony and seek production of documents and authorizes it to punish any firm or accountant failing to cooperate with an investigation. The PCAOB is to coordinate its investigations and disciplinary proceedings with those of the SEC. Importantly, Section 105 authorizes the Board to impose a wide variety of disciplinary or remedial sanctions, including (a) temporary suspension or permanent revocation of registration of firms; (b) temporary or permanent suspension or bar of an individual auditor from further association with a registered firm; (c) temporary of permanent limitations on activities of firms or individual accountants; (d) civil money penalties up to $100,000 for each violation by a natural person or $2,000,000 for a firm or, if violations are intentional or reckless or constitute repeated acts of negligence, these penalties may range up to $750,000 for individuals and $15,000,000 for firms; (e) censure; (f) required additional professional education or training; or (g) any other appropriate sanction. Accounting firms' supervisory personnel may be sanctioned (as may the firm) if they have failed reasonably to supervise individual auditors.

Section 106 recognizes that many foreign companies list their securities on American stock exchanges or otherwise offer shares to American investors and thereby come within the purview of American securities laws and must file certified financial statements with the SEC. These foreign companies are usually audited by foreign accounting firms and SOX states that they are subject to the Act just as are American accounting firms. Indeed, even if they do not issue audit reports but merely play "such a substantial role in the preparation and furnishing of such reports" that it would be consistent with the purposes of SOX to require them to register, the PCAOB may do so. When a foreign accounting firm certifies financial statements to be filed with the SEC or otherwise performs material accounting services in that connection, it is deemed thereby to have consented to produce audit workpapers in connection with a PCAOB investigation and to be subject to U.S. courts' orders in that regard. The

PCAOB and the SEC are granted authority by Section 106 to exempt foreign accounting firms from SOX's rules.

Section 107 gives the SEC oversight and enforcement authority over the PCAOB such that no rule of the Board becomes effective without prior approval of the Commission. The SEC cannot only amend any rules issued by the Board, it may review any sanctions that the Board imposes upon public accounting firms and their auditors.

Section 108 amends the 1933 Securities Act to authorize the SEC to recognize as "generally accepted" for the purpose of securities laws, any accounting principles established by standard setting bodies that meet certain criteria. As noted, the Commission seems satisfied to rely on the FASB.

Section 109 deals with funding of the PCAOB and envisions that much of its budget will come from fees imposed upon public companies and registered accounting firms.

Implications and Consequences. The audit profession will never be the same again. Public auditors have long lived within an extensive web of rules and regulations, and SEC rules and potential liability for violations of the federal securities laws are longstanding. That said, in the 1990s, given the political power of their organization, auditors could feel that to a large extent they controlled their environment. They had induced Congress to minimize their liability from securities class action suits. They had successfully lobbied to prevent strict accounting standards on such matters as mergers and stock options from becoming effective. They had several times stymied SEC reform by promising to cure any problems by self-regulation.

No more. For the foreseeable future, the auditors not only face all the old liabilities and SEC regulation, they also must check with PCAOB website on a frequent basis as that agency is churning out new rules in response to the Congressional mandate in Sections 101-109 of SOX. The new rules address how to register, what to disclose, fees charged, etc., etc. Then there are the annual inspections for the major firms, and yet another federal agency empowered to punish delinquent behavior.

Furthermore, it is the PCAOB, not the audit profession itself, establishing the most important new rules about how to conduct audits and report financial information.

No one reasonably believes that the PCAOB will go away any time soon, but many foreign accounting firms lobbied heartily for an exemption from PCAOB registration. Often they have claimed that they are already regulated in their home countries and that double registration would be inefficient. Although the SEC and PCAOB have offered conciliatory words to these foreign firms, the Board has nonetheless required them to register as envisioned in Section 106. However, in order to minimize duplicate regulation, the Board has agreed to defer to foreign regulatory agencies in inspection and enforcement activities if it believes that those foreign agencies are effectively doing their job.

Title II. Auditor Independence

After establishing regulatory oversight of the public accounting profession, Congress turned its attention to improving audit performance primarily by strengthening the independence of public company auditors.

Section 201.

The Problem. The large numbers of financial restatements and the hugely erroneous financial statements of Enron, WorldCom, Global Crossing and other companies lent credence to the long-standing arguments of many observers that the public accounting profession had used audit services as a loss-leader in order to garner consulting business with their audit clients. As consulting revenue soared, it logically became harder and harder for an auditor to stand up to an aggressive client that wished to flout the rules. There is substantial evidence that Arthur Andersen, for example, realized that Enron's accounting practices were questionable and that it faced substantial liability exposure. The firm's top brass decided, erroneously as it turned out, that the risk was worth it in light of the fact that AA was earning $50 million a year in revenue from Enron and that this number would likely soon rise to $100 million with the lion's share being consulting revenue.

Accounting firms often set up a client's internal controls, performed some of the internal control work, and then audited the process and result and certified them as satisfactory and accurate. When challenged regarding their independence, they claimed that their integrity was well established and that they would never tarnish it for a few measly consulting dollars. By dint of vigorous lobbying, the big public firms managed to write their own independence rules and cram them down the throat of a skeptical but politically weak SEC. The only compromise that the SEC managed to extract in the vigorous lobbying battle of 1999 was a requirement that public companies disclose how much they were paying in nonaudit fees to their audit firms.

Those disclosures showed that Big Accounting had been drastically underrepresenting the amount of nonaudit fees they were collecting from many, many audit clients. Before that information could even sink in, Enron had collapsed and daily revelations of new scandals made it difficult to believe that auditors' independence was not impaired by the selling of nonaudit services.

The Solution. Believing that auditors' provision of nonaudit services to public company audit clients had led them to be unduly client-friendly when performing audits, in Section 201 Congress required the PCAOB to ban provision of several types of nonaudit services to public company audit clients: "(1) bookkeeping or other services related to the accounting records or financial statements of the audit client; (2) financial information systems design and implementation; (3) appraisal or valuation services, fairness opinions, or contribution-in-kind reports; (4) actuarial services; (5) internal audit outsourcing services; (6) management functions or human resources; (7) broker or dealer, investment adviser, or investment banking services; and (9) any other services that the [PCAOB] determines, by regulation, is impermissible."

Any permitted nonaudit services are to be pre-approved by the client's audit committee. The PCAOB is authorized to approve necessary exemptions.

Although SOX does not require it, the SEC has issued rules providing that an auditor is not independent (and therefore its audits do not meet required standards) if auditors receive any compensation from the sale of consulting services.

Implications and Consequences. There is little doubt that consulting services dominated the attention of Big Accounting in the 1990s. Revenues from provision of information technology and other consulting services rose much more quickly than that from the two traditional major revenue streams for accounting firms—audit and tax services.

Sarbanes-Oxley returns accounting firms to their roots. Indeed, in light of the new limitations on provision of consulting services, three of the remaining Big Four accounting firms spun off their consulting branches. Occurring hot on the heels of the demise of Arthur Andersen, this created huge dislocation in the accounting profession.

Despite these spin-offs and the new rules, consulting will remain an important source of revenue for most accounting firms. SOX does nothing to prohibit accounting firms from providing consulting services to public companies that are not audit clients, or even to audit clients that happen to be private companies.

Many have argued that the PCAOB should exercise its discretion in subsection (9) of Section 201 by including tax preparation and/or tax planning services in the prohibited list. Although the matter remains under consideration and valid arguments can be made to support this view, it does not appear that the PCAOB will take this step any time soon. Such a move would, of course, cause further huge dislocations in the accounting profession.

Section 202.

The Problem. The independence of auditors is impaired, perhaps minimally and arguably necessarily, by the simple fact that the client pays the auditor's fee. More significantly, before Sarbanes-Oxley, the client's CEO and CFO functionally chose, evaluated, compensated, and fired the auditor. This gave these individual officers substantial leverage over the auditor. Indeed, several financial scandals involved situations where the auditors had become friendly with the client's executives. Some e-mails indicated that auditors were encouraged to be "team players," assisting the client to obtain its objectives rather than acting as a watchdog on behalf of investors as they are supposed to do.

The Solution. For this problem and others addressed in later provisions, Congress thought that increasing the authority of an "independent" body inside the corporation might improve auditor independence. Therefore, Section 202 provides that all auditing services and all permitted non-auditing services (with some de minimis exceptions) are to be *pre*-approved by the client company's audit committee, which is to composed entirely of independent directors.

Implications and Consequences. Henceforth, it is not company executives, but independent directors who will choose, compensate, and fire auditors. Already, in exercise of their discretion, several audit committees of major public companies have chosen to begin purchasing audit and tax services from separate accounting firms rather than following the traditional practice of having one accounting firm provide both. Such a separation, they believe, should not only improve the independence of the firm's auditor but also strengthen the appearance of independence and thereby give the investing public greater confidence in the company's certified financial statements.

Section 203.

The Problem. In Section 203 Congress again addresses the independence problem. Human nature is such that over time auditors may naturally develop good feelings for the client, hopes for its success, and friendships with client employees whom they encounter on a frequent basis. Several deficient audits in the Enron era happened after auditors and client employees socialized, went to ball games and shopping malls together, and even took vacations together. It is hard for an auditor to insist that a client take a position that will have immediate adverse consequences, including perhaps layoffs of friends who work for the client, when any consequences of allowing the client to fudge the rules may never occur and if they do it will be far in the future and the victims are currently nameless and faceless.

The Solution.   In Section 203, Congress requires public audit firms to rotate at least every five years the audit partner having primary responsibility for the audit and the audit partner responsible for reviewing the audit.

Implications and Consequences.   Many called for rotation of audit *firms*, not just audit partners. Five years of PricewaterhouseCoopers, then five years of Ernst & Young. Surely PwC will keep its eye on the ball better if it knows that within five years another audit firm will be examining its work.   Although firm rotation is required in some other countries, Congress decided it was a drastic change and, truthfully, there is little empirical evidence that it clearly improves auditor performance.   Therefore, Congress settled on this compromise. Still, an auditor such as David Duncan, who headed the Enron account for Arthur Andersen in Houston, can no longer view a particular client as his or her life's work. Five-on and five-off is the new rule for these top two partners. SEC rules allow other partners to audit on a 7-2-7 basis. They can audit a particularly client for seven years, then must rotate off for two years before returning for another seven (maximum).

Section 204.

The Problem.   Evidence disclosed in the Enron investigation indicated that the company's board of directors, which was generally composed of well-qualified and honest individuals, was poorly informed as to the aggressive nature of many of Enron's accounting tactics. Indeed, it appears that in many busted audits from the 1990s auditors and CEOs or CFOs went back and forth over proper accounting treatments. The CEO would wish to take an aggressive position. The auditor would resist and then ultimately cave in, perhaps in a desire to avoid angering the CEO and jeopardizing consulting revenue. Whatever the parties' motives, often the board of directors did not even know of the controversy.

The Solution.   Section 204 requires that each registered public accounting firm shall report *to the audit committee* of the board of directors regarding (a) all critical accounting policies and practices to be used (b) all alternative treatments discussed with management and their ramifications, and (c) other material communications between the auditor and management, such as a schedule of unadjusted differences.   SEC rules require a company to disclose substantial information about its "principal accountant" and the fees being paid for services.

Implications and Consequences.   This new requirement ensures that the board of directors will be in the loop. Had it been in place before the Enron scandal, Arthur Andersen would have had to call the audit committee's attention to the critical role special purpose entities were playing in allowing Enron to move debt off the books and could have made a more informed judgment as to the policy's wisdom.   AA would also have had to inform the audit committee when it jousted with CFO Andy Fastow over aggressive accounting treatments sought by Enron. In the future, boards will not be kept in the dark. Directors may not always make the right decision, but hopefully they will be aware of the implications of their decisions.

Section 205.

This is a nonsubstantive section that merely makes minor amendments to preexisting statutes to reconcile their language with SOX's.

Section 206.

The Problem.   When a staff auditor's supervising partner becomes CFO at the client, how is that staff auditor to comfortably make demands upon his or her old boss?

The Solution. To ameliorate this problem, Congress inserted a one-year waiting period in Section 206. No accounting firm is deemed independent if its auditors go to work for the client in any of several positions where they *participated in any capacity in the audit"* during the one-year period preceding the date of the initiation of the audit. The positions that cannot be assumed include (a) CEO, CFO, controller, CAO or any equivalent officers, (b) any financial oversight role, and (c) any person preparing financial statements.

Implications and Consequences. Auditors who begin and end their careers at a Big Four firm are in a distinct minority. A substantial percentage of accounting students (and young accountants) have viewed public accounting as a way station on the way to an attractive job in industry. Also, it certainly has not been unusual for small public companies especially to hire their CFO from their audit firm. Section 206 may prove a significant impediment to these past practices, because it really can prove to be more like a two-year cooling-off period given that the one-year period is that preceding the *beginning* of the audit. So if an audit partner was working on an audit cycle running from March of 2004 to February of 2005 and was approached by the client in June of 2004, he or she could not take a covered position with the client until after the March 2005-February 2006 cycle was completed. The auditor must perform and complete an entire cycle after its employee left before the former employee may join the client in a forbidden position.

Other impediments for auditors who might be approached by the client are AICPA ethics rules that require them to quit the audit until they have rejected the offer. They are to inform their superiors who can decide whether to adjust audit procedures. There are also ethical rules governing moves in the other direction, when employees of the client go to work for the auditor.

Section 207.

This provision simply orders the Comptroller General to conduct a study regarding the potential effects of a rule that ordered mandatory rotation of audit *firms*. The report concluded that this would be such a major change that it might be inefficient and potentially disruptive. It does not appear that rotation of firms will be required any time soon.

Sections 208 and 209.

Section 208 simply instructs the SEC to issue promptly issue final rules to carry out these provisions and Section 209 allows State regulatory authorities to make independent determinations of the standards they should apply to the small and medium nonregistered public accounting firms that they primarily supervise.

PART TWO: CORPORATE RESPONSIBILITY, DISCLOSURE, AND GOVERNANCE

Although the audit profession may certainly be faulted for the often-inadequate job many of its members did that contributed to the Enron era debacles, it cannot be forgotten that the primary wrongdoers were typically in company management. Accountants are mere gatekeepers. After addressing auditors' shortcomings, Congress turned directly to the companies themselves and set forth a broad range of rules addressing corporate disclosure, responsibility of officers and directors, and corporate governance reforms. These are included in Title III and Title IV.

Title III. Corporate Responsibility

Adam Smith pointed out the agency problem that exists in corporations, observing long ago that an agent watching over someone else's assets would never be as careful as a principal guarding his own. The development of corporate law over the past 200 hundred years has, in large part, been an attempt to solve this agency problem. How does the law prevent officers who run the corporation on behalf of its owners, the shareholders, from looting it? Certainly restrictions can be put in place, but too many will destroy the incentive of managers to work hard and take sensible risks. In Sarbanes-Oxley, Congress inserts federal influence into the corporate governance field, which has traditionally been occupied by the states.

Section 301.

The Problem. Corporate law has generally aimed to ameliorate the agency problem by providing a board of directors to monitor the officers who run the company day-to-day on behalf of the shareholders. But there is much evidence that during the dot.com boom director monitoring was insufficient. Judging from the covers of business periodicals during the time, it was the era of the CEO as movie star. Gary Winnick of Global Crossing profited more than $750 million while the company committed massive fraud to hide its failures. Dennis Kozlowski of Tyco, Richard Scrushy of HealthSouth, Ken Lay and Jeff Skilling of Enron, the Riga family of Adelphia, Bernie Ebbers of WorldCom (among other executives) became wealthy beyond the dream of avarice while running their companies into the ground. Executives of 25 companies whose stock price plummeted 75% or more between early 1999 and May 2002 walked away from their firms with $25 *billion* dollars in loans, stock options, and the like.

The Solution. Section 301 instructs the SEC to promulgate rules requiring national securities exchanges to refuse to list companies that did not comply with 301's requirements. Those requirements initially provided that audit committees of boards of directors would, as noted above, choose, compensate, oversee, and terminate their companies' auditors. More importantly, these audit committees must be composed entirely of independent directors, people who are not officers of the company and do not accept any consulting or advisory fees from the issuer or affiliate with the issuer or its subsidiaries in any significant way.

Keeping in mind Sherron Watkins and other whistleblowers of the Enron era (about whom we shall see more directly), Section 301 directs audit committees to establish procedures for receiving, retaining, and treating complaints about accounting procedures and internal controls and protecting the confidentiality of those complainants.

These are significant new responsibilities, and to ensure that the audit committee can carry them out, Section

301 grants audit committees the authority to engage lawyers and other advisers as needed and requires companies to provide audit committees with sufficient resources.

Implications and Consequences. The notion of an entirely independent and very powerful audit committee is relatively new to corporate governance. But now it is required for American public companies. It is quickly becoming "best practices" for other companies, including nonprofits. In the two years after passage of Sarbanes-Oxley, the percentage of CEOs who resigned or were forced out by their boards went up dramatically, indicating that directors are taking their responsibilities more seriously than before. Another sign is that on average directors are now spending 50% more time each month discharging their responsibilities than they did before SOX was passed.

One of SOX's great controversies is caused by the fact that many foreign companies list their securities on American stock exchanges and therefore are bound by the rule. Corporations of France, Germany, Japan and elsewhere have their own traditions of corporate governance that do not necessarily jibe with SOX's requirements. At this writing, the SEC is still working out just how much it intends to compromise on this issue to accommodate the variations found in other nations' practices. On the one hand, there is little empirical evidence that board independence dramatically improves corporate financial performance. On the other hand, there is *some* evidence, especially regarding the efficacy of independent audit committees, and there is a general trend across the world in the direction of increasing board independence.

Individuals who join the audit committee of the board of directors must keep in mind that greater responsibilities could lead to greater liabilities. That said, academic studies show that independent directors have virtually never had to pay judgments out of their own pockets for any conduct short of dishonesty or intentional breach of fiduciary duty. In the brief period of time following passage of SOX, there is no indication that it changes this fact. Still, pay for chairs of audit committees has risen substantially.

Section 302.

The Problem. Corporate management has primary responsibility for the preparation of financial statements and the creation of processes and systems of control to ensure that accurate information finds its way into those statements. That theoretical responsibility notwithstanding, in the white hot competition and excitement of the dot.com bubble, many corporate executives seemed to believe that it was their job not to produce accurate financial statements for the auditors to certify, but to bully the auditors into certifying as aggressive a set of financial statements as possible. Accuracy was not an important consideration if the auditor's certification could be obtained to "CY" the company's "A." In litigation, CEOs occasionally disclaimed any responsibility at all for financial statements, even though they had signed them.

The Solution. Section 302 requires each public company's CEO and CFO to certify that they have reviewed the quarterly and annual reports their companies file with the SEC, that based on their knowledge the reports do not contain any materially untrue statements or half-truths, and that based on their knowledge the financial information is fairly presented.

They must also certify that they are responsible for establishing and maintaining their company's internal financial controls, that they have designed such controls to ensure the relevant material information is made known to them, that they have recently evaluated the effectiveness of the internal controls, and that they have presented in the report their conclusions about the controls' effectiveness.

They must additionally certify that they have reported to the auditors and the audit committee regarding all significant deficiencies and material weaknesses in the controls and any fraud, whether or not material, that involves management or other employees playing a significant role in the internal controls.

Finally, the CEO and CFO must indicate whether or not there have been any significant post-evaluation changes in the controls that could significantly affect the controls.

Implications and Consequences. Many pre-SOX financial statements were signed by CEOs who meant to signify nothing more than "these financial statements may not be accurate, but they're not so bad that I couldn't talk my auditor into signing off on them." Since SOX, CEOs and CFOs risk considerable personal difficulties if they do not believe that the filings they sign are accurate and have not put into place reliable internal financial controls so that they can reasonably have some faith in their own beliefs. SOX returns to these internal financial controls in Section 404, as we shall see.

It is likely no coincidence that when this provision and Section 906 (which sets forth criminal penalties for false certification of financial statements in these filings) first applied to large public companies in August of 2002, HealthSouth's CFO resigned rather than certify the accuracy of HealthSouth's financial statements. His resignation tipped over the first domino, starting the process that within six months or so led to the uncovering of one of America's largest financial frauds. By August 2003, the SEC had nailed its first CEO and CFO for certifying reports without good faith.

Section 303.

The Problem. In several cases of busted audits in the Enron era scandals, there was evidence that auditors knew their clients were engaged in improper practices, confronted the clients, and were bullied into accepting the clients' wishes. CFOs were known to call the highest echelons of public accounting firms in order to force the removal of a recalcitrant audit partner or lower level auditor.

The Solution. Section 303 makes it unlawful for any officer, director or person acting under their direction to violate SEC rules by taking any action "to fraudulently influence, coerce, manipulate, or mislead" an auditor for the purpose of rendering financial statements misleading. In civil proceedings, only the SEC can enforce the rule—investors cannot sue.

Implications and Consequences. In 1977, Congress passed the Foreign Corrupt Practices Act (FCPA) in order to stop American companies from bribing foreign government officials to obtain and retain business. The Act also included provisions to improve accounting practices because, for some reason, public companies' financial statements seldom carried an entry for "bribes paid" even though many such bribes were huge in size. One of the accounting provisions made it unlawful to lie to an outside auditor. Section 303 repeats that prohibition and similarly prohibits more subtle acts, including fraudulently influencing and coercing. Some auditors have told the author that before Sarbanes-Oxley, some client officers seemed to believe that their job was not to produce accurate financial statements, but as aggressive a set of financial statements as they could bully their outside auditor into accepting. After passage of Section 303, corporate officers have tended to be decidedly less aggressive in their confrontations with auditors over proper practices. Even company officers who believe they are in the right must be careful.

Section 304.

The Problem. Particularly galling to shareholders of Enron, Adelphia, WorldCom, Global Crossing and many others was the fact that not only did they lose most or all of their investment in these companies when it was discovered that earnings had been massively overstated or losses had been hidden, but officers of the companies did not seem to suffer commensurately. They kept the bonuses and stock options they had been granted in reward for earnings that later proved illusory. They kept the profits they gained from selling stock at high prices before the securities fraud was discovered and prices plummeted. Between January 2000 and August 2002, the stock market dropped $5.5 trillion in value while top insiders of Enron, Qwest, Global Crossing and others sold $1.7 billion worth of shares, *and* often delayed reporting. The disparity between the fate of innocent investors and that of executive wrongdoers struck Congress as unfair.

The Solution. Section 304 requires the CEOs and CFOs (only) of public companies (domestic and foreign) to reimburse their companies for any bonus or other incentive-based compensation earned, or trading profits received, in the twelve-month period that follows the first issuance or filing with the SEC of financial statements that are subsequently restated "as a result of misconduct."

Implications and Consequences. Among several unanswered questions about this provision is how "misconduct" should be construed. Does it require fraudulent intent or just recklessness or even some lesser wrong? Also, must the misconduct referred to in the statute be that of the CEO and/or CFO, or is the misconduct of underlings that the CEO and CFO are unaware of sufficient to require disgorgement? One view is that the CEO and CFO should not have to disgorge profits if they were not personally guilty of wrongdoing. The other view is that if such misstatements happened on their watch, they should have to disgorge even if they lacked personal culpability. After all, they profited from illusory earnings. The statute has no clear answer to these questions, and legal commentators have disagreed as to the proper interpretation.

Section 305.

The Problem. By their acts of extreme greed, some notorious characters in the Enron era scandals proved their utter unfitness to ever hold a position of responsibility in a public company.

The Solution. Section 305 reduces the showing needed to bar individuals from ever serving as officers or directors of public companies from "substantial unfitness" to mere "unfitness."

Implications and Consequences. In its experience, the SEC has run across many serial conmen. For example, one family had enough money to buy control of a small public company. It would then install family members in corporate positions, greatly increase prior salaries, and essentially loot the company. With those profits it would buy a stake in a slightly larger company and repeat the process. Around 1990,

Congress granted the SEC authority to request that federal courts to bar from office in public companies people who had demonstrated their "substantial unfitness" to hold such positions. As we shall see presently, SOX's Section 1105 authorizes the SEC to issue such bars without going to court and the Commission has not been reticent to do so.

Section 306.

The Problem. At a critical time in Enron's demise, its pension plan was scheduled to change administrators and during that changeover most of its employees were prohibited from trading or "blacked out." They could not sell their Enron shares as the stock price continued its march south. Executives of the company, on the other hand, could bail out as the corporate parachute collapsed.

The Solution. In Section 306, Congress provided that the SEC should issue rules making it unlawful for any director or executive officer of an issuer, to buy or sell company securities during any pension plan black-out period. The SEC did so in Regulation Blackout Trading Restriction ("Reg BTR"), which requires disgorgement of any profit realized, irrespective of whether the director or officer acted with bad intent. Any shareholder may file such a suit on behalf of the issuing company if it fails to bring suit itself. Reg BTR defines "blackout period" to mean any period of more than three consecutive business days during which more than 50% of the participants of a pension plan are prevented from trading.

Implications and Consequences. The obvious unfairness of lower level employees being locked into a stock in free fall while the top brass escape the crash motivated congressional action. The new rule is fair, but based largely on urban myth. By the time the Enron black-out hit, the stock price had already dropped from nearly $90/share to $13/share and declined only another $3/share or so during the blackout period.

Section 307.

The Problem. Where were the lawyers? Among the gatekeepers who seemed to have failed shareholders during the Enron era scandals were attorneys. Like auditors, they often seemed to team up with companies' managers to skirt financial regulations and others laws. They often seemed to forget that their true clients were the corporations and their shareholders who ultimately suffered when falsely inflated stock prices fell back to earth. When a company like Enron sought to move huge amounts of debt off the books, the directors signed off because the lawyers and auditors had signed off. The lawyers signed off because the auditors did. The auditors signed off because the lawyers did. No one took responsibility.

The Solution. Section 307 ordered the SEC to issue rules containing minimum standards for attorneys representing public companies as both in-house and outside counsel. The Commission issued rules requiring attorneys to report material violations of state and federal laws "up the ladder." If the initial persons to whom they report do not respond appropriately, attorneys have the obligation to report all the way to the board of directors (but not outside the corporation). The rules also instruct companies in how to handle these reports, suggest that companies might create a new committee for the board of directors (the qualified legal compliance committee) to accept these reports, and specify when foreign attorneys must make such reports.

Implications and Consequences. Attorneys certainly got off lightly compared to accountants at the hands of Sarbanes-Oxley. The SEC has thus far rejected suggestions that attorneys should have to report violations to the SEC or short of that, have to resign their positions ("noisy withdrawals") if the company does not react properly to their complaints. Those who argued that attorneys are in a different position than auditors won the day. They contended that while auditors are watchdogs in a supposedly adversarial situation with the corporate client, attorneys are advocates for the client who cannot do their job if they are forced to rat it out to the feds.

Section 308.

The Problem. Too many times shareholders victimized by frauds never received any meaningful compensation, even if the SEC brought charges against the wrongdoers and often even when they were plaintiffs in class action lawsuits who prevailed in litigation.

In insider trading cases, for example, statutes passed in the 1980s forced wrongdoers to pay fines which went into the U.S. Treasury. They also had to disgorge profits earned which theoretically went into a fund to reimburse shareholders who sold while the insider bought or bought while the insider sold. However, the IRS often got to that money first (inside traders seldom declare their illegal profits as income) and other times judges decided that it would be too difficult to determine who was trading opposite the insider and ordered the disgorged funds to be paid into the Treasury, leaving shareholders high and dry.

The Solution. Section 308 orders that civil penalties shall, on the motion or direction of the SEC, be added to disgorged funds for the benefit of the victims rather than being paid into the U.S. Treasury. It also requires the SEC to study enforcement actions over the five years preceding SOX's passage to determine the best processes to fairly provide restitution to injured investors.

Implications and Consequences. Pursuant to this "Fair Fund" provision, the SEC has been fairly aggressive in seeking disgorgements that will be paid to injured investors. The SEC report commissioned by Section 308 found that among obstacles to efficient disgorgement were difficulties in collecting from individuals who had been ordered to disgorge but might be in bankruptcy (or jail), administrative costs to create and administer disgorgement plans, and the fact that the defendant's profits might be only a small percentage of the losses caused by his lies. The Commission recommended further legislation, such as a law excluding securities cases from the state law homestead exemption but such changes have not yet been seriously considered.

Title IV—Enhanced Financial Disclosures

Although several provisions of the first three titles of Sarbanes-Oxley aim at enhancing the accuracy and reliability of the financial statements of public companies, Title IV adds several additional provisions.

Section 401.

The Problem. Among the financial skullduggery of the Enron era were (a) Enron moving large amounts of debt off the books, (b) Enron and other companies using special purpose entities (SPEs) to manipulate their financial status, and (c) wide use by many companies of pro forma financial statements (euphemistically called "everything but the bad stuff") that presented a much more favorable picture of their financial condition than GAAP-compliant financial statements. The top NASDAQ 100 firms overstated actual audited profits in their pro forma earnings announcements by $100 billion in just the first nine months of 2001. The top 500 S&P firms overstated income by 35% on average in their pro forma report.

The Solution. Section 401 instructs the SEC to issue rules requiring that quarterly and annual financial reports filed with the SEC disclose all material off-balance sheet transactions, arrangements, obligations, and other relationships with unconsolidated entities that might have a material impact on the financial statement.

It also orders the SEC to study the use of SPEs and how best to manage the situation so that they are not used to facilitate misleading off-balance sheet transactions.

Finally, it instructs the SEC to issue rules requiring that pro forma financial statements be presented in a manner that does not contain a material misstatement or half truth and be reconciled with the financial conditions and results of operations under GAAP so that investors can readily detect the differences. In response, the SEC issued Regulation G which imposes a broad range of limitations upon the use of pro forma results, including a requirement that public companies disclosing such results include the most directly comparable GAAP financial measures and a reconciliation of the two.

Implications and Consequences. There are many legitimate uses for off-balance sheet transactions as well as special purpose entities, so it is not surprising that use of these devices has continued after enactment of SOX. Nonetheless, the SEC is taking these new rules seriously; in August of 2004 it launched a new investigation because it was dissatisfied with companies' compliance with a new FASB accounting rule known as FIN 46, aimed at minimizing the amount of debt that can be moved off balance sheet.

Many have questioned why the SEC does not ban pro forma reporting altogether, rather than just corral its use through Reg G. Many companies are continuing to issue pro forma reports, but hopefully Reg G makes them more meaningful.

Section 402.

The Problem. As noted earlier, many CEOs got very wealthy during the Enron era, even as shareholders suffered. Not only did they receive huge salaries, big bonuses, and plentiful stock options, they often were granted loans by their companies. Tyco loaned CEO Dennis Kozlowski several hundred million dollars. Adelphia loaned its founding family a couple of billion. When the companies went under, those loans mostly went unrepaid. The average large company loaned almost a million dollars a year to top executives.

The Solution. Section 402 amends the 1934 Securities Exchange Act to prohibit public companies from making personal loans to executive officers and directors, with some minor exceptions such as home improvement loans made in the ordinary course of business.

The Implications. This provision has been a bit of a nightmare for corporate officers and attorneys, in part because it is a little unclear. Assume that an executive travels on company business. Normally the executive would pay the expenses out of her own pocket and then be reimbursed by the company, but because this is a particularly expensive trip the company fronted the money to the executive. Is this an improper "personal" loan? What about "split dollar" insurance policies, arrangements where employers pay part or all of the premiums of life insurance premiums for employees and later assign their cash portions to the employee? The IRS treats these as loans, but the SEC has not yet ruled as to how these common policies should be treated under SOX.

Note that while SOX outlaws loans, it does not ban outright gifts of those same sums. However, those would have to be disclosed and presumably directors will be reticent to abuse their authority to grant gifts. (However, compensation for the average CEO is now 530 times higher than that of the average company worker, so directors aren't showing much reticence in granting compensation).

Section 403.

The Problem. Hearings leading to passage of the 1934 Securities Exchange Act convinced Congress that insider trading was a serious concern. It responded by passing Section 16(a) which required officers, directors, and holders of 10% of a company's stock—the three categories of people that Congress presumed had natural access to inside information—to file reports with the SEC regarding their trades in company stock. If those reports showed that the insiders had transactions within six months of each other that resulted in a profit or avoided a loss, the company or shareholders on its behalf, could sue under Section 16(b) to have those profits or avoided losses disgorged to the company.

Under Section 16(a) most transactions had to be reported within ten days of the beginning of the following month. In other words, a transaction on March 1 had to be reported by April 10. However, certain transactions with the company did not have to be reported until 45 days into the following fiscal year. So, a February 1 transaction involving a company whose fiscal year did not end until December 31 might not have to be reported until February 15 of the following year.

During 2001, Enron's Ken Lay engaged in many sales of Enron stock that did not have to be disclosed and remained unknown until early 2002. Rather stale news by then.

The Solution. Section 403 amends Section 16(a) to require that most transactions by insiders be electronically filed with the SEC within *two* business days (with some exceptions). Any company maintaining a corporate website must post these filings on their sites by the end of the business day. The rule does not apply to non-U.S. issuers.

Implications and Consequences. Filing 16(a) reports is burdensome and even before SOX dramatically shortened the filing deadline, it seemed that many officers and directors filed their reports tardily or not at all. The SEC reacted to this by requiring companies to disclose these violators in their annual statements (assuming this would embarrass the companies into policing their own) and by occasionally imposing substantial fines upon violators. In the post-Enron era, insiders and their companies must be especially sensitive to the need to file promptly.

Section 404 .

The Problem. In Section 404 Congress again addressed the problem of the accuracy and reliability of public companies' financial statements. Section 302 requires CEOs and CFOs to certify that to their knowledge the reports their companies file with the SEC are accurate. But how are they to know that the information upon which they predicate their beliefs is reliable?

Perhaps more to the point, company executives, notably Jeff Skilling, former CEO of Enron, testified before Congress that they just had no idea that their companies' financial statements were off by *billions* of dollars. Congress sought to deprive these executives of plausible deniability.

The Solution. Complementing Section 302, Section 404 requires each annual report to contain an "internal control report" stating the responsibility of management for establishing and maintaining an adequate internal control structure so that accurate financial statements could be produced and containing an assessment, as of the end of the

most recent fiscal year, of the effectiveness of the internal
control structure and procedures. Section 404 also requires
auditors to audit the internal control assessment of the
company as well as the financial statements.

Implications and Consequences. Section 404 is the
most controversial of all the provisions of Sarbanes-Oxley.
During the Watergate era when the scandals that led to
passage of the Foreign Corrupt Practices Act erupted, many
top executives of leading companies testified before Congress
that they had no idea how low-level underlings had laid their
hands on millions of dollars of company assets to pay bribes
to foreign government officials in order to land contracts for
the companies. The FCPA required public companies to
institute effective internal controls to stop the bribes and to
make executives accountable. Section 404 goes further, but
has similar goals.

Section 404 focuses on internal *financial* controls, so
that information used to produce financial statements is
reliable. "Best practices" may include:

- A disclosure committee to review procedures and
  processes
- A disclosure coordinator, to be the one person any one
  in the organization can go to with a question and who
  tries to keep everyone on the same page
- A time line and responsibility chart
- Subcertifications, where lower level employees certify
  the accuracy of the information they send up the line
- Codes of conduct for all accounting and financial
  employees
- Lots of consultation with internal audit and outside
  advisors (many consultants are currently specializing
  in helping companies set up effective internal
  controls), and
- Established documentation procedures

Many companies have indicated that Section 404 is no
problem for them. They are well managed and already have
such controls in place so that they can know where they are
making money and where they are losing money. For
example, Dell Computer expected to spend only $250,000,

mostly documenting already existing controls. Other companies, however, have found it quite expensive to set up, document, and evaluate such controls. General Electric claims it spent $30 million in so doing, and one study found an average cost of $3.1 million for 224 public companies surveyed. Much of this expense, of course, is a one time only cost to set up and document the controls. But ongoing maintenance and evaluation will not be cheap. It also costs money for outside auditors to audit these controls, perhaps 20-100% of the pre-404 audit fees, although one estimate is that average public company audit fees before SOX were only $1/20^{th}$ of 1 percent of company revenues.

Even companies that have found 404 to be expensive to implement have often realized large cost savings because the new controls revealed inefficiencies or frauds that were previously undetectable. Some controllers of public companies have used Section 404's mandates to gain permission and resources to institute changes that they had wanted to make for years. Some British companies coming within SOX's reach announced that they intended to gain efficiency by instituting the controls, although they expressed doubt that monetary savings would exceed costs of implementation.

Section 405. Section 405 simply states that Sections 401, 402, and 404 do not apply to registered investment companies (mutual funds).

Section 406.
    The Problem. Enron CFO Andy Fastow not only obliterated the line between proper and improper accounting procedures, he feathered his own nest to the tune of $40 million or so in hidden or otherwise improper compensation. He was far from the only CFO during the Enron era who fudged financial numbers and profited unfairly at the expense of shareholders.
    The Solution. Section 406 requires public companies to disclose in their filings with the SEC whether or not they have adopted a code of ethics for senior financial officers

(CFOs, comptrollers, principal accounting officers, and others performing similar functions). If they have not adopted such a code, they are to give the reason why. The code is to address such matters as conflicts of interest, accurate financial reporting, and compliance with governmental rules and regulations.

Implications and Consequences. The potential embarrassment of explaining why they have not adopted a code of ethics for senior financial officers has prompted most companies to adopt one. However, as Enron proved, having a snappy code of ethics does not mean much in practice if it is observed mainly in the breach. Unless corporate management exhibits a sincere commitment to ethical conduct, the code becomes merely a piece of paper.

Section 407.

The Problem. In retrospect, it appears that boards of directors were often overmatched during the Enron era. Not only were they often faced with dishonesty from the managers they were supposed to monitor, occasionally it appears that they did not appreciate the facts and figures right in front of them. More sophisticated monitors might have detected some of the "funny" accounting and overly aggressive financial maneuvers.

The Solution. Section 407 requires that at least one member of the audit committee be a "financial expert," someone who through education and experience--coming from experience as a public accountant, auditor, CFO, comptroller, or a position involving performance of similar functions—has (a) an understanding of GAAP and financial statements, (b) experience in preparing or auditing financial statements of comparable companies and application of such principals in connection with accounting for estimates, accruals and reserves, (c) experience with internal auditing controls, and (d) an understanding of audit committee functions.

Implications and Consequences. Having elevated the role of the audit committee to the pinnacle of importance in the corporate governance process, Congress sought to give it the tools to do its job not only by ensuring that all its members are independent (Section 301), but also that at least one of them has the financial sophistication and experience to truly serve the monitoring function. Retired CFOs and auditors have become hot tickets for board of director positions. The new responsibilities (and potential liabilities) and the stricter qualifications mean that it is taking longer than ever before to fill director vacancies and search firms are making lots of money in the field.

Section 408.

The Problem. For many years, the SEC has been understaffed and underfunded. Many of the Senators and Representatives that jumped on the SOX bandwagon after so many scandals unfolded on nationwide television had been happy to virtually starve the agency for many years. Because of its precarious funding, the SEC did not review nearly as many company filings in the 1990s as it had in previous years. Without SEC review, financial problems are more likely to escape notice for a longer time.

The Solution. Section 408 instructs the SEC to review periodic disclosures made by public companies "on a regular and systematic basis for the protection of investors." In scheduling reviews, the SEC is instructed to consider, among other factors, whether issuers (a) have restated financial results; (b) have experienced relatively significant market volatility; (c) have large market cap; and (d) are emerging companies with disparities in P/E ratios. In any event, each company's filings should be reviewed at least every three years.

Implications and Consequences. The first implication of this requirement is that the SEC needs more money and staff, and that is provided in a different SOX provision (Sec. 601). After two years, the SEC is bringing more enforcement actions than ever before and many of the violations likely would not have been noticed had the SEC been doing more reviews. The Commission recently found a company that submitted financial statements supposedly certified by a Big Four firm. In fact, the Big Four firm had not signed off on the financials; the company just pretended so. Absent an inspection of the company's filing, this misrepresentation might not have been detected.

Section 409.

The Problem. The common law provides that companies do not have a duty to disclose new information unless (a) the law requires it, (b) they need to do so in order to correct a previous error, or (c) insider trading is occurring. If the companies are not under an obligation to file an annual report (10-K), quarterly report (10-Q), or interim report (8-K) or if they are not engaging in a public offering, tender offer or proxy solicitation, then they generally have no duty to disclose adverse information that investors would like to know. The current disclosure system is one of *periodic* disclosure. Many believe that it dates from a different era, before computers, and that relatively *continuous* disclosure is now possible and perhaps should be mandated.

The Solution. Section 409 amends the 1934 Act to require public companies to disclose to the public on a "rapid and current" basis information that the SEC determines is necessary or useful for the protection of investors and in the public interest.

Implications and Consequences. The SEC is currently studying the feasibility of real-time disclosure. To move toward that goal, the Commission reduced the amount of time after period end in which companies have to file annual and quarterly reports and substantially amended the rules for interim 8-K disclosures, broadening the number of items that must be disclosed without waiting for the next quarterly or annual filing deadline, increasing the amount of information that must be disclosed regarding some of the categories, and shortening the deadline for 8-K filing to just four business days from the occurrence of the significant event.

Among the items that must now be disclosed in 8-K reports within four business days of occurrence are: (a) entry into or termination of a material definitive agreement not made in the ordinary course of business; (b) a completed acquisition or disposition of significant amount of assets not made in the ordinary course of business; (c) public announcement by the company of material nonpublic information regarding the company's operations or financial condition; (d) creation of a material direct (or of an indirect *off-balance sheet*--remember Enron) financial obligation; (e) an event, such as a default that causes acceleration of material financial obligations; (f) determination that impairment of a material asset, such as goodwill, is required under GAAP; (g) notice that its securities are likely to be delisted by a stock exchange or NASDAQ; (h) sale of equity securities unless a registration statement is filed with the SEC; (i) any material modification of the rights of shareholders; (j) any restatement of financial statements earlier filed; (k) changes in control; and (l) departure of directors or top officers. The total number of triggering events requiring an 8-K riling rose from 12 to 22, leading to an expectation that the number of 8-K reports filed every year with the SEC will rise from 80,000 to 140,000 in the near future. In other words, companies must pay attention for they will have to file roughly twice as many 8-Ks as they had to file before SOX.

PART THREE: WALL STREET REFORMS

Title V—Analyst Conflicts of Interest

Section 501.

The Problem. Securities analysts often find themselves in difficult conflicts of interest. Theoretically they objectively analyze stocks and give investors unbiased information regarding investment choices. However, most analysts work for investment banks which would dearly love to provide investment-banking services for the companies that issue the stock the analysts evaluate. Therefore, the securities analysts' employers place various forms of pressure upon the analysts to discourage them from giving negative evaluations of stocks. The employers can give investment bankers veto power over analysts' recommendations. They can compensate analysts based not on how accurate their recommendations are, but upon how much investment banking business they bring in. They can even fire analysts who displease clients and potential clients by negatively evaluating their stock.

So much of this pressure was applied in the 1990s that analysts were seldom rewarded for being correct and many stopped trying to be. Henry Blodgett publicly touted shares that he disparaged in private e-mails as "junk" and "crap." He occasionally threatened to "call 'em like he saw 'em" notwithstanding the consequences for his employer Merrill Lynch's investment banking fees, but never quite managed to muster the courage to do so.

There is evidence that Citibank analyst Jack Grubman changed a recommendation so that his firm could better compete for some underwriting business in exchange for Citibank making a million dollar contribution to a private school Grubman wished to induce to admit his children. It is undeniable that Grubman was in bed with investment banking client WorldCom.

Blodgett and Grubman were scarcely alone. Of 33,169 buy, sell or hold recommendations made in 1999, only 125 (0.3%) were pure sells.

Revelation of the Grubman and Blodget shenanigans forced changes even before SOX. Just a month before SOX was enacted, the SEC approved amendments to NASD and NYSE rules that, among other requirements, (a) limited relationships and communications between an investment bank's securities analysts and its investment bankers; (b) prohibited investment banks from compensating analysts based on specific investment banking transactions; (c) imposed requirements preventing firms from promising favorable research to potential clients or threatening them with unfavorable research; and (d) restricted personal trading by research analysts.

Also just before SOX was passed, the SEC, New York Attorney General Eliot Spitzer, an association of state securities regulators (NASAA), and the exchanges announced a "Global Settlement" with major ten major brokerage houses (such as Merrill Lynch, Bear Stearns, and Goldman Sachs), in which the houses agreed to pay $875 million in fines and disgorgement, $80 million to fund and promote investor education, and $432.5 million to fund independence securities research. Also, the Global Settlement sought to strengthen the "firewall" between securities analysts and investment bankers in a number of ways.

The Solution. In Section 501, Congress implicitly approved the exchanges' amendments and the Global Settlement's provisions summarized above, and directed the SEC to adopt additional rules to address conflicts of interest and to adopt or require the exchanges to adopt helpful rules. The SEC adopted Regulation Analyst Certification ("Reg AC") which, among other requirements, provides that analysts must certify (a) that they actually believe in the report and recommendations they are making, and (b) that no part of their compensation is linked to specific recommendations or views.

The SEC later directed NYSE and NASD to issue even more rules, including two that (a) further separated analyst compensation from investment banking by removing investment bankers from compensation committees evaluating analysts, and (b) prohibited analysts from issuing positive research reports or reiterating "buy" recommendations ("booster shots") near the date of expiration of a "lock-up" agreement that has prevented insider from selling their shares.

Implications and Consequences. Rule 501 sought to drastically revamp the manner in which Wall Street has done business in recent years. Certainly, independent research firms were given a shot in the arm by the Global Settlement's provisions.

Investment banks claimed that this new regime would stifle the distribution of helpful information for investors, but they had claimed the same thing a few years earlier when the SEC promulgated Regulation FD (aimed at leveling the playing field between lay investors and institutional investors) and most academic studies done of Reg FD indicate that this did not occur. Most evidence indicates that Reg FD created more fairness without reducing disclosure. Only time will tell whether Rule 501 will do the same.

PART FOUR: SEC REFORMS AND FURTHER STUDY

Title VI—Commission Resources and Authority

In Title VI, Congress gave the SEC additional authority to sanction wrongdoers and sought to fund the agency at an appropriate level.

Rule 601.

The Problem.   For many years before the Enron scandal, the SEC was clearly underfunded and understaffed. As the economy grew and the number of public companies expanded and their filings with the Commission grew exponentially, SEC employee numbers were nearly flat. Because of staff and budget shortages, more and more filings went unreviewed.   Civil proceedings and criminal actions (referred to the Department of Justice for action) were prioritized and only the most pressing were pursued.

The Solution. Congress authorized large increases in the SEC's budget, from $438 million in fiscal 2002 to $776 million in fiscal 2003.

Implications and Consequences.   Although fiscal complications prevented much of the promised funding from every arriving, the SEC's budget has been substantially increased. The Commission has hired more staff and in early 2002 it examined the annual reports of the largest American companies for the first time in years. Both the Commission bringing administrative and civil actions and the Department of Justice (DOJ) bringing criminal cases, have been more active. For example, in July 2002, the Corporate Fraud Task Force was formed and within two years had secured convictions or guilty pleas from 44 CEOs in white-collar cases. In fiscal 2002, the SEC's Division of Enforcement opened 479 investigations, instituted 317 civil proceedings, and 281 administrative proceedings. The following year, it instituted a record 679 enforcement actions. SOX has created a more robust SEC.

Section 602

The Problem. As noted earlier, accountants and attorneys did not acquit themselves impressively during the Enron era. The SEC has long had authority to discipline accountants and attorneys who practice before it, and has often suspended auditors from auditing public companies and attorneys from representing them, sometimes temporarily and occasionally permanently. The SEC's rules implementing this authority were often challenged in court.

The Solution. In Section 602, Congress reinforced some key SEC rules by making them part of the statute. The law creates a new Section 4C in the 1934 Act that allows the SEC to censure any person or deny them the privilege of appearing or practicing before the Commission if it finds after notice and hearing that the person (1) does not possess the requisite qualifications to represent others; (2) is lacking in character or integrity or has engaged in unethical or *improper professional conduct*, or (3) has willfully violated or willfully aided and abetted a violation of the securities laws.

The statute then states that with respect to public accounting firms specifically, the term "improper professional conduct" means both (1) intentional or knowing conduct (including recklessness) that results in violation of professional standards, and (2) *negligent* conduct in the form of (A) a single instance of highly unreasonable conduct that results in a violation of professional standards in a situation where the accountant knows or should know that heightened scrutiny is warranted, or (B) repeated instances of unreasonable conduct indicating a lack of competence.

Implications and Consequences. The SEC had long maintained that it had authority to discipline attorneys and accountants for mere negligence. After losing a court battle over a rule ultimately deemed too vague, the SEC issued a rule pretty much identical to that summarized in the second paragraph above. Some had argued that the SEC did not have authority to issue the rule and did not have authority to punish mere negligence. Congress has rendered that debate moot by codifying the SEC rule.

Sections 603 and 604.

These two provisions received little attention as Sarbanes-Oxley was passed and virtually none since. Section 603 broadens judicial authority to bar persons guilty of misconduct from participating in a penny stock offering and 604 increases the SEC's authority to bar or suspend persons from working for broker-dealers or investment advisers, particularly if they have are already in trouble with state authorities.

Title VII—Studies and Reports

In passing Sarbanes-Oxley, political pressure arising from a steady drumbeat of disclosures of financial fraud in 2001 and 2002 caused Congress to act much quicker than is typical for a legislative body. Showing some caution, Congress left several matters for further study.

Section 701.

The Problem. In a wave of consolidations, the Big Eight accounting firms that came to dominate the world market for accounting in the 1970s and 1980s became the Big Six and then the Big Five and then, finally, the Big Four when Arthur Andersen went under. Can there be adequate competition in pricing and service quality when only four firms audit around 80% of all public companies and 99% of all public company sales?

The Solution. Section 701 ordered the Government Accounting Office (GAO) to undertake a study of the consolidation in accounting firms and consider its implications.

Implications and Consequences. The GAO report found increased consolidation but no clear evidence of a decrease in competition resulting yet. Although fees for audits are increasing, a number of other factors (including increased responsibilities under Sarbanes-Oxley) are probably a greater cause than higher concentration in the audit firm market. The report also found that none of the second-tier accounting firms, such as Grant Thornton or McGladrey & Pullen, are poised to join the Big Four and thereby provide more competition at the top.

Section 702.

The Problem. In addition to attorneys, directors, auditors, and stock analysts, credit rating agencies such as Standard & Poors are supposed to serve as gatekeepers protecting investors. During the dot.com bubble, they seem to have performed poorly as well, often giving companies high ratings until right after the company tanked.

The Solution. Section 702 orders the SEC to study the credit agencies and to issue a report regarding their role in the market, impediments to accurate appraisal, barriers to market entry, conflicts of interest, and related factors.

Implications and Consequences. The SEC's initial report called for more study, but raised concerns over ratings agencies' inadequate disclosure of the bases for and assumptions underlying their evaluations. The Commission also deemed conflicts of interest worthy of further study, especially because agencies rely on issuer fees for large portions of their revenue and recently have begun offering ancillary services to those same issuers (just as auditors did, ruining their reputation for objectivity).

Section 703.

The Problem. In the early 1990s, the Supreme Court issued a decision in the *Central Bank* case that overturned many years of lower court precedent by holding that there was no aiding and abetting cause of action under the federal securities laws' main antifraud provision, Section 10(b) of the '34 Act. For years, plaintiff investors had sued fraudulent companies and their officers as primary violators of 10(b), but usually sued auditors and attorneys on theories of secondary liability such as aiding and abetting. In the PSLRA of 1995, Congress restored the authority of the SEC to bring aiding and abetting actions, but refused to extend the right to private shareholders suing for damages. In light of the poor performance of attorneys and auditors during the Enron era, Congress considered overruling *Central Bank* regarding private damage plaintiffs as well, but decided not to do so.

The Solution. Instead, Congress ordered the SEC to perform a study looking at the January 1, 1998 to December 31, 2001 period to determine what types of professionals (auditors, investment bankers, investment advisers, brokers, dealers, attorneys, etc.) practicing before the commission had been sanctioned, which types of violations they had committed, and what types of sanctions had been applied. It appeared that Congress wanted additional information before deciding whether to reinstate the private cause of action for aiding and abetting.

Implications and Consequences. The study found that during the four-year period studied, 1,596 securities professionals were found to have violated federal securities laws. The most common defendants were broker-dealer employees. The most common types of cases involved securities offerings and fraud against broker-dealer customers and the most commonly violated sections were the general antifraud provisions of the '33 and '34 Acts. Only 13 individuals were charged solely as aiders and abettors, indicating perhaps that it is not necessary to change the law to increase aiding and abetting exposure. It is very unlikely that Congress will act again to overrule *Central Bank.*

Section 704.

The Problem. Given the vast problems with securities fraud, often in the form of false financial statements, Congress was concerned that the SOX provisions it enacted in June 2001 might be inadequate.

The Solution. Section 704 orders the SEC to review and analyze all its enforcement actions in the area of reporting requirements and financial restatements and to submit the information to Congress for possible further legislative action.

Implications and Consequences. In the five-year period covered by the SEC's report, it had filed 515 enforcement actions for financial reporting and disclosure violations. Members of senior management of issuers were the most frequent defendants and improper revenue recognition was the most frequent charge. The SEC recommended more uniform reporting of restatements of financial statements and improved Management Discussion & Analysis (MD&A) disclosure as well as increased SEC investigative authority. No action has yet been taken on these recommendations.

Section 705.

The Problem. Investment banks loved Enron, Global Crossing, and several other of the high-flying companies that crashed so hard at the turn of the century. They made millions of dollars in fees helping these entities raise money. Indeed, they were advisers, underwriters, provided stock analysts, counterparties in suspicious transactions, and in other ways were heavily involved with the companies. In certain transactions with Enron, it appeared that investment banks did deals that knowingly aided Enron in temporarily moving debt off its books or temporarily showing illusory income.

The Solution. Congress ordered the Comptroller General of the United States to conduct a study on whether investment banks had assisted public companies in manipulating their earnings and obfuscating their true financial condition, with particular attention to the Enron and Global Crossing cases.

Implications and Consequences. The GAO report was issued while lawsuits over the investment banks' role in several Enron era scandals were ongoing. Therefore, the report often used the word "allegedly." It found that investment banks claimed innocence, but were strengthening their internal reviews and risk assessments to minimize the chance of suffering a repeat of the reputational and financial injury they suffered when Enron, Global Crossing and other companies crumbled. The report also noted that in the future regulators should be alert to the incentive investment banks may have to participate in questionable transactions with clients they would like to sell consulting services to.

PART FOUR: NEW CRIMES AND PUNISHMENTS

A not uncommon congressional response to a problem is to create new crimes and to increase the punishment for violations of existing criminal provisions. SOX is typical in this regard.

Title VIII—Corporate and Criminal Fraud Accountability

Section 801.

Section 801 simply gives Title VIII the title of the "Corporate and Criminal Fraud Accountability Act of 2002."

Section 802

The Problem.   When Sarbanes-Oxley was passed, Arthur Andersen was being tried for allegedly shredding huge amounts of documents in order to hide its complicity in the Enron fraud.   A jury agreed with the prosecutors that a somewhat obscure message from an AA attorney in Chicago was a covert instruction to destroy evidence.

Certainly, evidence destruction is appealing to a person under investigation and it is a concern for law enforcement.   Note that Martha Stewart was convicted not of insider trading, but of tampering with evidence.   Frank Quattrone, one of the richest and most influential investment bankers of the dot.com boom was similarly convicted of ordering subordinates to destroy documents rather than of a substantive securities fraud offense.

Unfortunately, the statutes on the books that were used to convict Arthur Andersen were a little unclear and Congress worried that defendants might be escape conviction via limitations in the coverage of existing statutes.

The Solution. Section 802 added two new statutes punishing alteration of documents. The first [codified at 18 U.S.C. Sec. 1519] addresses destruction, alteration, and falsification of records in federal investigations and bankruptcy, imposing a criminal penalty of up to 20 years imprisonment. The provision is not limited to securities fraud cases and does not require that an indictment have been issued or even that an investigation be pending.

The second [18 U.S.C. Sec. 1520] requires auditors who audit a reporting company to maintain all audit or review workpapers for 5 years, but by rule the SEC changed this to 7 years from the conclusion of the review in order to be consistent with new auditing standards. The SEC rules define "workpapers" broadly and the statute imposes a potential punishment of up to 10 years imprisonment for knowing and willful violation.

Implications and Consequences. As Martha Stewart, Frank Quattrone, and Arthur Andersen demonstrated, people who learn that they are under investigation often respond by destroying documents. These provisions mean that people who do so may face stiffer penalties for the destruction than they would have faced for the underlying substantive offense had they been convicted. It has been pointed out that in the current environment, if someone is caught with a bag of shredded documents, that bag might as well contain cocaine.

Soon after SOX was passed, DOJ began indicting individuals under Sec. 1519. In a pending case, DOJ charged that an auditor destroyed documents in an effort to prevent "smart ass lawyers" from looking over his audit team's work. In another, a mutual fund vice-president received a criminal conviction, a civil fine of $400,000 and a lifetime industry ban for deleting e-mails and directing his staff to lie to the SEC.

The auditors' document retention responsibilities in Sec. 1520 will likely be expensive, with some large firms claiming the costs could exceed a million dollars a year.

Section 803.

The Problem. Persons who commit securities fraud and are fined by state or federal authorities, ordered to disgorge profits, or lose civil damage judgments may seek to avoid paying them by declaring bankruptcy and discharging those obligations.

The Solution. In Section 803, Congress made judgments incurred via securities fraud violations nondischargeable in bankruptcy.

Implications and Consequences. This provision should help the SEC and private plaintiffs to collect fines imposed and judgments obtained.

Section 804.

The Problem. Section 10(b) had no express statute of limitations. Therefore, the Supreme Court judicially required plaintiffs to meet two deadlines. First, they had to file suit before one year had passed from when they discovered, or in the exercise of due diligence should have discovered, the fraud. Second, they also had to file within three years of when the fraud actually occurred. If they missed either deadline, their lawsuit was barred, and many were.

The Solution. Section 804 extends the statute of limitations in securities fraud cases from 1-year/3-years to 2 years/5years. Plaintiffs must now sue within two years of discovery of the fraud and within five years of the fraud's occurrence.

Implications and Consequences. This new provision will undoubtedly prevent many securities fraud lawsuits from being dismissed that would have been dismissed before Sarbanes-Oxley. Most courts have held that this extended limitations period does not apply to 1933 Act provisions or to lawsuits filed before SOX was passed.

Section 805.

The Problem. Although there were already securities fraud and obstruction of justice statutes on the books, they did not prevent the Enron and related frauds.

The Solution. Thinking that more severe penalties might do a better job of deterring fraud, Congress in Section 805 ordered the United States Sentencing Commission to review and amend the Federal Sentencing Guidelines to ensure that punishments for obstruction of justice and abuses of trust are sufficient to deter and punish that activity.

Implications and Consequences. Because of new guidelines, potential wrongdoers should be more worried than ever before about-facing lengthy incarceration.

Section 806.

The Problem. Many of the Enron era frauds involved many individuals. Often many were actively involved in the fraudulent scheme. Many more knew what was going on. A precious few blew the whistle. Sherron Watkins of Enron and Cynthia Cooper of WorldCom did and became Time magazine's People of the Year. Because employees want to be team players and loyal to their company, they find it difficult to tattle on co-workers and superiors. Whistle blowing is additionally discouraged by the adverse consequences that can quickly follow. When Sherron Watkins wrote her famous memo to Enron's CEO Ken Lay warning that their company was about to implode in a wave of accounting scandals, there was a memo on his desk within 48 hours explaining that if Enron fired her for whistle blowing, Watkins was not protected under Texas state law.

The Solution. Section 806 is just one of three provisions Congress inserted in SOX designed to encourage and protect whistleblowers. We have already seen that Section 301 requires audit committees to set up procedures for handling whistleblower complaints. Section 806 provides a civil damages action for public company whistleblowers who suffer retaliation for providing information in an investigation or participating as a witness or otherwise in a proceeding involving federal securities law violations. The statute sets up a procedure involving an administrative complaint initially filed with the Secretary of Labor.

Implications and Consequences. Today Sherron Watkins would be protected by this provision, and it is clear that every company and every supervisor must take whistle blowing extremely seriously. Procedures must be established and scrupulously followed. In the first 18 months after SOX was passed, whistleblowers had filed 170 charges with the Department of Labor. In early 2004, the first two decisions on the merits of these claims were issued. The first found in favor of a former CFO of a bank holding company who had repeatedly complained to management about financial reporting practices before being terminated. The Administrative Law Judge ordered the CFO's reinstatement. The second ruling found for a former equity research analyst who claimed that she was terminated after refusing to upgrade her evaluation of the stock of a company that her securities firm wanted to do business with.

Section 807.

The Problem. Although Section 10(b) is the strongest pro-plaintiff anti-fraud provision in the world, it contains several elements and plaintiffs in civil cases and prosecutors in criminal cases must satisfy them all to prevail. One element that is tricky is that the defendant's fraud must have occurred "in connection with" a purchase or sale of securities. Some courts have construed this requirement in a restrictive manner making it hard for prosecutors (and civil plaintiffs).

The Solution. Section 807 adds a new securities fraud provision to the federal criminal code (Title 18 of the U.S. Code). The language in subsection (1) is quite similar to the broad antifraud wording of Section 10(b), but omits the "in connection with" requirement. Subsection (2) adds something that is not in Section 10(b)—punishment for "obtain[ing], by means of false or fraudulent pretenses, representations, or promises, any money or property in connection with the purchase or sale of any security" of a public company. The penalty for violation could be a fine and imprisonment for as long as 25 years.

Implications and Consequences. It was already a crime to intentionally violation Section 10(b), but that criminal provision was in the federal securities code; now there is a similar provision in the federal criminal code. It reduces the prosecutor's burden and slightly broadens the types of activity that can be punished. Nonetheless, most observers believe that in the near future, prosecutors will continue to emphasize the tried and true Section 10(b), which has a well-defined body of case law clarifying its parameters.

Title IX—White-Collar Crime Penalty Enhancements

In Title IX, Congress again returned to its theory that harsher penalties and more criminal statutes will improve deterrence.

Section 901-905.

Section 901 simply names Title IX the "White-Collar Crime Penalty Enhancement Act of 2002."

Section 902 adds subjects people who *conspire* to commit mail, wire, or securities fraud to the same punishment as those who commit the substantive offense.

Section 903 increases the maximum potential jail term for wire fraud and mail fraud (which are often involved in securities fraud) from 5 years to 20 years.

Section 904 increases the maximum penalties for criminal violations of the Employee Retirement Income Security Act (ERISA).

Section 905 directs the United States Sentencing Commission to review and amend sentencing guidelines for white-collar offenses, with a view to increasing the punishment.

Section 906.

The Problem. The problem again is inaccurate reports filed with the SEC.

The Solution. In Section 302, Sarbanes-Oxley required CEOs and CFOs to certify their belief in the accuracy of the quarterly and annual reports filed with the SEC. Section 906 adds a criminal provision punishing these officers if they intentionally certify SEC filings containing financial statements (Section 302 is not limited to just financial statements). "Knowing" violations are punishable by fines of up to $1 million and imprisonment of up to 10 years. "Willful" violations are punishable by fines of up to $5 million and imprisonment of up to 20 years.

Implications and Consequences. As with Section 302, this provision should clearly focus the minds of CEOs and CFOs and remind them every quarter that their job is to sign accurate financial statements, not just financial statements that the auditors have signed off on. The law has never been particularly clear on the difference between "knowing" violations and "willful" violations. Perhaps some day a case brought under this provision will provide clarity.

Sections 302 and 906 clearly require attention to Section 404—the setting up of internal financial controls. Without an adequate set of controls, how can officers certify the truthfulness and accuracy of the filings they sign in good faith? The SEC and DOJ have signaled that CEOs and CFOs have responsibility to investigate hints of significant employee misconduct that might undermine the accuracy of these filings.

PART FIVE: CORPORATE TAX RETURNS

Title X—Corporate Tax Returns

Section 1001.

Not really relevant to securities law, but perhaps pertinent to the Enron scandal, Title X expresses the "sense of the Senate" that CEOs should sign corporate income tax returns.

PART SIX: CORPORATE FRAUD AND ACCOUNTABILITY

The final title of Sarbanes-Oxley contains miscellaneous provisions that often overlap many earlier provisions.

Title XI—Corporate Fraud and Accountability

Section 1101.

Section 1101 simply provides the title for this section—"The Corporate Fraud Accountability Act of 2002."

Section 1102.

The Problem. Congress returns again to the problem of obstruction of justice.

The Solution. Section 1102 adds another criminal provision, punishing anyone who "corruptly (1) alters, destroys, mutilates, or conceals a record, document, or other object, or attempts to do so, with the intent to impair the object's integrity or availability for use in an official proceeding; or (2) otherwise obstructs, influences, or impedes any official proceeding, or attempts to do so." The punishment is a fine and/or imprisonment of up to 20 years.

Implications and Consequences. Along with the two provisions added in Section 802 relating to destruction of documents, this provision adds a broad and powerful weapon to the prosecutor's quiver. Companies must seriously consider putting policies in place regarding document retention and destruction to minimize the chance that their employees might violate these provisions. Arthur Andersen's fate should provide incentive enough.

Section 1103.

The Problem. It is not always easy to determine quickly who is involved in fraudulent activity. While the SEC is investigating, defendants' funds have a way of disappearing. Occasionally a company under SEC investigation will pay large bonuses to officers who just might have had something to do with the fraud.

The Solution. Section 1103 authorizes the SEC to freeze temporarily the funds of a company when it seems likely that it will make "extraordinary payments" to directors, officers, controlling persons, or others.

Implications and Consequences. The SEC has often used this power. In its first application, the Commission ordered escrowed $37.64 million in cash payments made by Gemstar-TV Guide International to its former CEO and CFO. Those officers later convinced a court to release the funds on grounds that the payments were not "extraordinary." A dissenting judge said: "If these mega-suspicious payments were not 'extraordinary,' the word needs either to be redefined or to be out of our dictionaries....One would not expect benefits like these to be flowing from corporate assets to executives resigning under fire. This scenario is not business as usual. It appears to be looting."

The SEC has also frozen funds at other prominent companies, including HealthSouth, WorldCom, and Vivendi.

Section 1104.

Section 1104 is yet another directive to the United States Sentencing Commission urging it to immediately review sentencing guidelines with respect to securities fraud and related offenses. Recommendations for changes focus on whether a defendant corporation has promoted "an organizational culture that encourages a commitment to compliance with the law." SOX seeks to force corporations to be proactive in developing effective legal compliance programs to prevent misconduct by employees.

Section 1105.

This section authorizes the SEC to issue administratively orders that temporarily or permanently ban individuals from serving as officers or directors of public companies. As noted by in the discussion of Section 305, the SEC has not been reticent about using this power, especially since Section 305 lowered the necessary showing from "substantial unfitness" to mere "unfitness." In 2001, the SEC requested 51 bars. That number rose to 126 in 2002 and to 170 in 2003. For example, Sam Waksal, former top officer of ImClone and key figure in the Martha Stewart insider trading scandal, has been barred.

Section 1106.

Section 1106 increased the criminal penalties for intentional violation of provisions of the '34 Act. For individual violators, Congress raised the maximum fine from one million dollars to five million dollars and the maximum imprisonment from not more than 10 years to not more than 20 years. For firms, the maximum fine was raised from $2.5 million dollars to $25 million dollars.

Section 1107.

The Problem. After ordering audit committees to set up a mechanism for allowing whistleblower complaints to be heard (Section 301) and providing whistleblowers a right to sue for civil damages (Section 806), Congress returned to the whistleblower issue a third time.

The Solution. Section 1107 makes it a crime punishable by fine and/or imprisonment of not more than 10 years to retaliate against an informant who provided truthful information relating to the commission of *any* federal offense to a law enforcement officer.

Implications and Consequences. No criminal charges have yet been brought under Section 1107's provisions, but every single supervisor of employees in America must be cognizant of its provisions and penalties. The rule is very broad, covering whistle blowing regarding any federal offense, not just securities fraud and applying to all companies including nonprofits, not just public companies. Again, companies must install and follow procedures for handling whistleblower complaints. The civil damage and criminal penalty consequences of improperly retaliating against a whistleblower are fearsome.

CONCLUSION

Sarbanes-Oxley is a landmark piece of federal regulation that will remain controversial for years. Among other features, it created a new federal agency (the PCAOB), forced corporations at home and abroad to revamp their governance practices, made over the accounting industry, protected whistleblowers, created many new crimes (especially for document destruction), and increased punishment for violation of many existing ones.

SOX's immediate purpose was to restore confidence in the securities markets. Both investor reaction as reflected in empirical studies of trading and investor surveys indicate that it was generally successful. Congress seems to have reached that same conclusion and therefore is unlikely to tinker substantially with SOX any time soon.

Despite loud complaining at home and abroad about its burdens, a basic acceptance of Sarbanes-Oxley's provisions seems to be settling in as companies and accounting firms realize that many of its provisions, while disruptive and expensive (its provisions have apparently doubled the average cost of "being public" to $2.5 million annually), may well constitute "best practices" in corporate governance and accounting firm operation so far as the current state of knowledge can ascertain. Thus, few of the many American companies that have threatened to "go private" to avoid SOX's burdens have actually done so. And virtually none of the many foreign companies that have threatened to leave American capital markets have executed their threats. Ultimately, Sarbanes-Oxley may prove to be exactly what one CEO termed it: "Healthy, but a pain in the ass."

Robert Prentice is a University Distinguished Teaching Professor and Ed & Molly Smith Professor of Business Law at the McCombs School of Business at the University of Texas at Austin. He has published a textbook on securities regulation and written nearly fifty law review articles on securities law and related topics.